Tom Paxton
Comedians & Angels

Contents

Piano/Vocal arrangements by John Nicholas

Cherry Lane Music Company
Director of Publications/Project Editor: Mark Phillips
Project Coordinator: Rebecca Skidmore

ISBN 978-1-160378-052-0

Visit our website at www.cherrylaneprint.com

Tom Paxton

Despite more than four decades of recording and performing, the only sign that Tom Paxton may be slowing down a bit is that his past is catching up to him. In 2005 he received a Lifetime Achievement Award for Songwriting at BBC Radio 2's Folk Awards in London. The following year he was the recipient of a 2006 Lifetime Achievement Award from the North American Folk Music and Dance Alliance, honoring "those who have devoted their life's work and talent to the advancement of folk music and dance." And in January 2007 the British Parliament paid official tribute to his life and work, with former Labour leader Lord Neil Kinnock describing Paxton, a perennial UK favorite, as "one of the great folksingers…

the real voice of America [who] speaks for decent Americans."

In the 45 years since he started performing regularly in New York's Greenwich Village, Paxton has earned his place as one of the great "singing journalists" in the tradition of Woody Guthrie, Pete Seeger, Phil Ochs, and the early Bob Dylan; as an early pioneer in the performing of original, personal compositions rather than traditional folk songs; and as one of our finest contemporary songwriters. Although his own records have never sold in the quantities they merited, such Paxton originals as "The Last Thing on My Mind," "The Marvelous Toy," and "My Ramblin' Boy" reached a wider public through cover versions by more "commercial" folk acts—the Chad Mitchell Trio; Peter, Paul & Mary; and the Kingston Trio. The Fireballs had a Top 10 hit with Tom's good-timey "Bottle of Wine" in 1968. As early as 1969, Paxton's status as an underappreciated craftsman was noted in Lillian Roxon's groundbreaking, first-of-its-kind *Rock Encyclopedia*: "The trouble with Tom Paxton is that he's been too good too long and people take him for granted."

But sometimes good things do come to those who wait. In addition to the recent honors mentioned above, Paxton has enjoyed long-overdue appreciation in the 21st century. In 2002 he received a Lifetime Achievement Award from the American Society of Composers, Artists and Publishers (ASCAP), and three "Wammies" (Washington, DC, Area Music Awards) as Best Male Vocalist in both the Traditional Folk and Children's Music categories and for Best Traditional Folk Recording of the Year for *Under American Skies*," his duo CD with frequent collaborator Anne Hills. His 2001 CD *Your Shoes, My Shoes* was a Grammy finalist in the Children Music category, and 2002's *Looking for the Moon* was a Grammy finalist as Best Contemporary Folk Album.

Born in Chicago on Halloween in 1937 but transplanted with his family to tiny Bristow, Oklahoma, at age 10, Paxton caught the music bug for R&B, classical, and folk music in junior high school. Although he entered the University of Oklahoma as a drama major, his attraction to folk music blossomed and he acquired an acoustic guitar as a sophomore. "By the time I got out of college…I loved this music so much that I had to try it…I had undergone a chromosomal change after hearing the *Weavers at Carnegie Hall* album."

As a fresh-faced army reservist stationed at New Jersey's Fort Dix, Paxton was within commuting distance of Greenwich Village, where he slept on friends' floors and performed in small "basket houses" for change. After his six-month stint in the reserves ended, he became a Village fixture. One of the first of

the new crop of folksingers to write original material, Paxton—alongside Bob Dylan, Phil Ochs, Fred Neil, and Dave Van Ronk—helped open the floodgates of the singer-songwriter movement. As the outspoken musical activist Steve Earle recently told *No Depression* magazine, "The singer-songwriter thing came out of the folk movement. The first guys who wrote their own songs were Dylan and Tom Paxton. They were both really good." In San Francisco during a 1963 West Coast tour, Tom "discovered" another young singer-songwriter, (future Appleseed Recordings label-mate) Eric Andersen, and sent him back east to join the musical party.

In 1964 Paxton was signed to Elektra Records, the flagship label for creative folk music, and recorded *Ramblin' Boy*, his first of an estimated 35 or 40 albums. The following year, Paxton made his first of many annual tours of Great Britain. At the 1969 Isle of Wight Festival in the UK, Paxton's performance stole the show from the most popular rock bands of the day and solidified his English fan base. He lived in London during the early '70s, when he collaborated with various British folk stars (including Ralph McTell and Danny Thompson) and recorded his first of many albums of children's songs.

After returning to the States, Paxton became a beloved constant on the folk circuit. He has been acclaimed for the depth and wit of his songs and for the humor he brings to his dozens of yearly performances. Tom is a delightful storyteller with or without a guitar in his hands, and since 1987 he has written the text for more than a dozen children's books. Whether Tom sings of love (as on *Comedians & Angels*), of topical events (as in his ongoing series of "short shelf-life songs" frequently posted for free download on his website), of toys and measles and holidays (as on his children's CDs), or of the everyday people and place that surround him, what's left of the "real" America couldn't have a better spokesman.

ABOUT THE ALBUM
by Tom Paxton

We recorded this album (I still call them that) in Nashville the week of September 24, 2007. That sounds a little flat—a little cut and dried—so let me put it this way: We had a full-out blast for five days in Nashville! We played all day with the best musicians in the world! This the most fun you can ever possibly have on this planet. Much better.

My producer, Jim Rooney, works efficiently. Nothing is rushed, but neither does he waste a lot of time. You might like to hear how it works. The musicians gather around me with the yellow legal pads they find on their music stands when they arrive. As I sing through a

song they've never heard before, they scribble in what is known as the Nashville Number System, a shorthand for the chords they hear in the song. When I finish they compare notes and when they all agree on the chord progression we play through the song together. It is uncanny how completely they are already into the song. Jim says, "Let's try one," and we do. It seldom takes more than a few takes, and it's worth noting that with each time through they generally play less. They know what's extraneous and out it goes. They are simply amazing.

Easygoing is how you'd describe Jim Rooney 45 years ago and now. He always knew what the joke was, and if you asked him, he'd tell you. He was one of those left-handed guitar players, and he played with Bill Keith a lot, singing songs like Bobby Charles' *Tennessee Blues*. He told me of how, though he'd gone to school at Amherst, he always loved what was called, in those days, "hillbilly music."

He ran the Club 47 in Cambridge in the early '60s until it closed, spent time in Woodstock, and then moved down to Nashville, where he spent the next several decades working in country music with people like Allen Reynolds, and producing, writing, publishing, and recording people like Nanci Griffith, Iris DeMent, Barry & Holly Tashian, and, beginning in 1994, me.

From day one in Cowboy Jack Clement's attic recording studio in Nashville back in 1994, I knew I had found my producer. Jim had assembled an unbeatable band: Mark Howard, guitar; Roy Husky Jr., bass; Stuart Duncan, mandolin and fiddle; Richard Bailey, banjo; Joey Miskulin, piano and accordion; and on and on. All brilliant and interested, and many of them with us on this project, as well. We've now done four albums together, this being the fourth. God willing, there will be more.

How Beautiful upon the Mountain
Reading through the Bible (cramming for my finals?), I came across a stunning line in Isaiah 52:7. Loosely paraphrased, it became the chorus of this song. The chorus came almost instantaneously; the verses were much slower to emerge. After many false starts I found myself reading the chorus again. "Those who walk in peace." *Of course.* I've known *them* for 50 years—marched with them, mourned, sung, and laughed with them. If you're reading this, you are more than likely one of them. They (and you) were why I wrote this song.

Out on the Ocean
Written with my friend George Wurzbach of Brooklyn, this song is something of a departure, I guess. But damn, I like to sing it!

What a Friend You Are
So old, it's new again. I wrote this song while my family and I were living in London in the very early '70s. Midge was having real health problems and she was very much on my mind as I wrote it. I talk a lot about how my songs aren't really personal. The hell they're not. This is how I still feel about my partner. As I said elsewhere, she knows why.

When We Were Good
And you know what? We still are.

The First Song Is for You
Midge had still not heard this song when, in Belfast on a UK tour, I left the hotel to do an evening news program to promote the concert. I told her to be sure to watch the show, knowing that, for good reason, she didn't always bother. When they asked me for a song, I looked into the camera and saw her. She knew it was her song. I really don't mind—I love, actually—giving Midge the credit for so much of what I've done. I write for her; I prize her reaction when I've come up with a winner. She makes me a winner.

And If It's Not True
Like an earlier song, "My Pony Knows the Way," this song is sung in the voice of an imagined character. Midge and I have amused ourselves trying to describe how we think he would dress. I see old but good corduroy trousers and a worn but beautifully cut tweed jacket. For her it's completely different. He emerged slowly in the notebook and it took several rewrites to bring him into focus. The real fun nowadays is in the rewriting.

Bad Old Days
Back in 1980 I was recording for folk labels like Mountain Railroad and Flying Fish and working with Bob Gibson on all those projects. There was a folk club in Chicago called Earl of Old Town and I sang this song for Bob in

a broom closet they called a "dressing room." We recorded it right away. Nana Mouskouri recorded it in English, French, and German. I stuck to English.

Reason to Be
The joke in our family is that instead of buying my wife, Midge, a present, I write her a song. You'll have to ask her. I do know that she's a never-failing source of inspiration—my partner, my editor, my best friend.

I Like the Way You Look
How do these things happen? I will plug along day after day, writing nothing much worth looking at, and then for no reason a lyric like this shows up in the notebook. Why? Who knows? Something I ate—maybe (with me, always a lively possibility). I took to it at once. It was a new kind of lyric for me, and the tune just shouldered all other possible melodies aside.

A Long Way from Your Mountain
Midge and I were in Blue Hill, Maine, visiting our friends Noel and Betty Stookey in their home overlooking Penobscot Bay. As the earliest riser, I took my coffee and my notebook out onto the deck and sat totally absorbed in the view, which seemingly changed every five minutes. I finally turned to the notebook and wrote a lyric that I showed to Midge, but I didn't get around to trying to find a melody. A year later we were driving to Maine again and I was playing a tape sent to me by my sometime collaborator, Susan Graham White. On it she played piano or guitar and sang "la la" melodies. We worked that way often, and on this occasion Midge suddenly said, "This tune sounds like it would work with the lyric you wrote at the Stookey's. She was right; it took only a minor change or two and there it was—and here it is.

Home to Me (Is Anywhere You Are)
I've recorded this song before, most notably with my friends Anne Hills and the late Bob

Gibson on our 1985 concert CD, *Best of Friends* (Appleseed).

Jennifer and Kate
I wrote songs for my daughters when each was about three years old. Their songs are different, but then, so are my daughters. Jennifer was always the scholar, doing more on every school project than was required, and it seemed logical that she would go on to take a Ph.D. from Harvard in medieval history and hold a teaching position at Georgetown University in Washington, DC. Along the way she married Steve Silvia, also an academic and a splendid husband and father, and they have given us three grandsons: Christopher, Sean, and Peter. Kate was a people person from day one and has enlivened all our lives—sometimes greatly so! She finished college at Skidmore and went into public relations—a perfect fit for her. She also became a superb chef, which makes her dad a happy man.

Dance in the Kitchen
Go on! Do it! Good song on the radio, your honey right there. Irresistible combination, wouldn't you say?

You Are Love
I hear reports of this song being performed at weddings, and that pleases me greatly. Others tell me they interpret this song religiously; why not? We can never write, read, sing, or paint enough about love—whatever it means to us.

Comedians and Angels
In the old days there was a bar on Christopher Street, just east of Seventh Avenue. It was called the Lion's Head and it was only coincidental that its near neighbor down the street was the famed Stonewall, the gay bar that launched the Gay Pride movement with a memorable riot.

That's another story. The Lion's Head was mainly a writer's bar—a watering hole for journalists, sports writers, novelists manqué

and actual, and for an interesting sprinkling of poets. I spent perhaps a few more evenings there than was strictly wise. The walls were hung with framed covers of the books produced by the patrons, proving that they actually wrote something *before* bragging about it.

In its entire lifespan the Lion's Head allowed no jukebox to pollute its atmosphere. When you consider that the boys who supplied jukeboxes were, to put it mildly, "connected," you really had to honor their principles.

No one missed the recorded yowlings of teenage wonders. There was a peace to the place; conversation was valued, practiced, and enjoyed. The only alternative to the spoken voice was the voice raised in song. Of that there was often a lot. On a given evening, after midnight, say, one might hear such worthies as the Clancy Brothers, with or without Tommy Makem, sitting in the side room running through their limitless repertoire. Dave Van Ronk knew at least as many songs as they did, as did occasional visitor Theo Bikel. None of them blushed to add to the musical pot. It has occurred to the perceptive reader by now that I couldn't know this without having put in my share of time and song.

These are great memories.

How Beautiful upon the Mountain

Words and Music by
Tom Paxton

Moderately slow, in 2

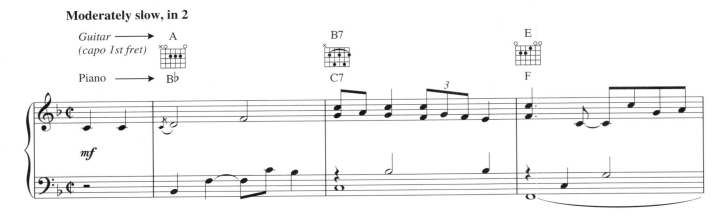

How beau - ti - ful up - on ___ the moun -

tain   are the   steps   of   those who walk in

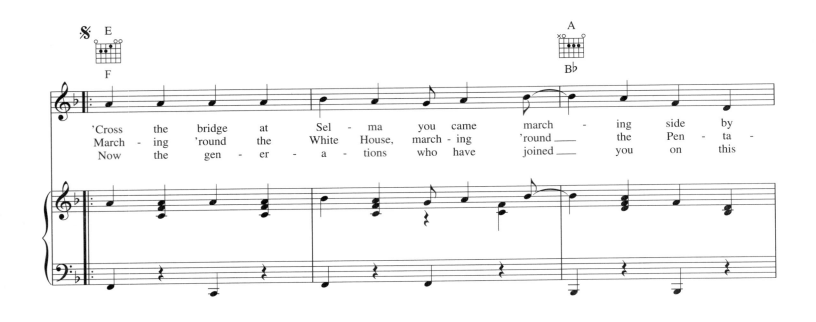

'Cross the bridge at Sel - ma you came march - ing side by
March - ing 'round the White House, march - ing 'round ___ the Pen - ta -
Now the gen - er - a - tions who have joined ___ you on this

side, in your eyes ___ a new world on the
gon, march - ing 'round ___ the might - y mis - sile
road look - ing to you ___ with pow - er in their

way. ___ Hope was in your heart ___
plants, ___ speak - ing truth to pow -
eyes. ___ Now you know the torch ___

10

and   jus - tice   would   not   be   de - nied. ____
er,   sing - ing   peace   in   Bab - y - lon, ____
has   passed   as   they   pick   up   the   load. ____

You   sang   "we   shall   o - ver - come ____ some - day." ____
ask - ing   us,   Why   not   give   peace ____ a   chance? ____
Now   you   see   their   eyes   are   on ____ the   prize. ____

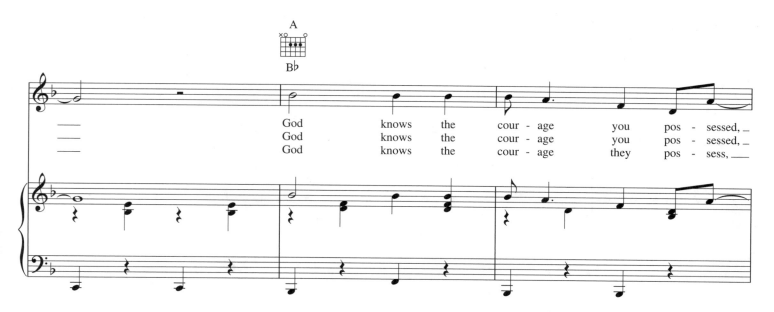

____   God   knows   the   cour - age   you   pos - sessed, _
____   God   knows   the   cour - age   you   pos - sessed, _
____   God   knows   the   cour - age   they   pos - sess, ____

D.S. al Coda

peace, _____ are the steps of those __

__ who walk in peace! _____

14

Out on the Ocean

Words and Music by
Tom Paxton

What a Friend You Are

Words and Music by
Tom Paxton

break a - way. You said you'd stay, and

here you are, _____ here you are. ___

here you are. What a spe - cial friend __ you are! __

rit.

22

When We Were Good

Words and Music by
Tom Paxton

The First Song Is for You

Words and Music by
Tom Paxton

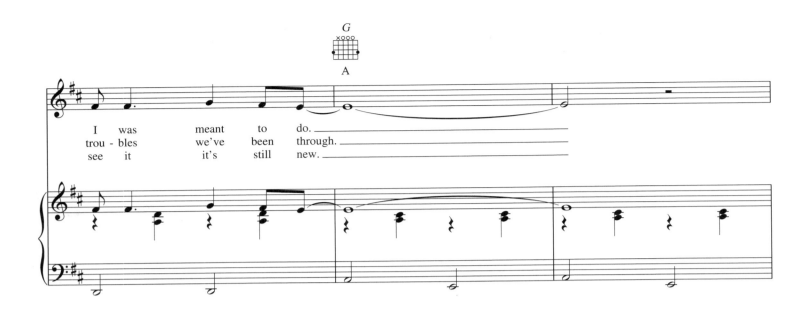

I was   meant   to   do. _____
trou - bles   we've   been   through. _____
see   it   it's   still   new. _____

With - out   know - ing   how, ___ I   find   I   write ___ your   name   a - gain.
Nev - er   would - 've   come ___ so   far   with - out ___ a   love   so   strong.
I   might   write   a   thou - sand   songs,   but   as ___ I   write   them   all,

Oh,   it's   al - ways   true: the   first ___ song   is   for   you.
So   it's   al - ways   true: the   first ___ song   is   for   you.
it - 'll   still ___ be   true: the   first ___ song   is   for   you.

And If It's Not True

Words and Music by
Tom Paxton

Most of my eve - nings I spend on my own, lis - t'ning to Span - ish _____ gui -
Some - times on Sun - days I stroll through the park, down by the car - ou -
Ah! The Im - pres - sion - ists up at the Met; I vis - it when - ev - er _____ I

tars.
sel,
can.

Next year, I say, Bar - ce - lo - na for me, and
hear - ing the chil - dren ride 'round in de - light to a
It's "Bon - jour" to Vin - cent, _ "Bra - vo" to Hen - ri, but the

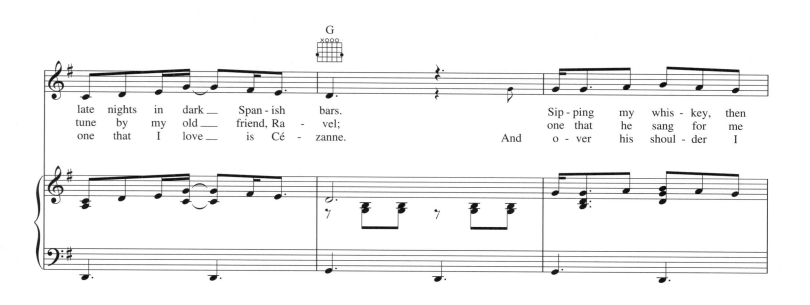

late nights in dark _ Span - ish bars.
tune by my old _ friend, Ra - vel;
one that I love _ is Cé - zanne.

Sip - ping my whis - key, then
one that he sang for me
And o - ver his shoul - der I

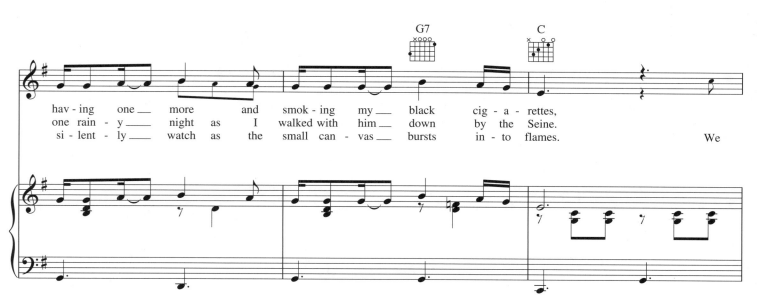

hav - ing one _ more and smok - ing my _ black cig - a - rettes,
one rain - y _ night as I walked with him _ down by the Seine.
si - lent - ly _ watch as the small can - vas _ bursts in - to flames.

We

Bad Old Days

Words and Music by
Tom Paxton

ger's in the tell - ing; _____ I'm tempt - ed to be bright, __ when the

truth is, they were bad ___ old days; did - n't have to turn out right. I

love you more than morn - ing, _____ and part of the rea - son why __ is you helped __

D.S. al Coda I

_____ me kiss those bad old days ___ good - bye. ___ Oh, I won -

39

Reason to Be

Words and Music by
Tom Paxton

My love lies be - side   me,   breath - ing soft and
My love finds me wait - ing   when   the dawn comes
She will rise and wan - der   through   the long green

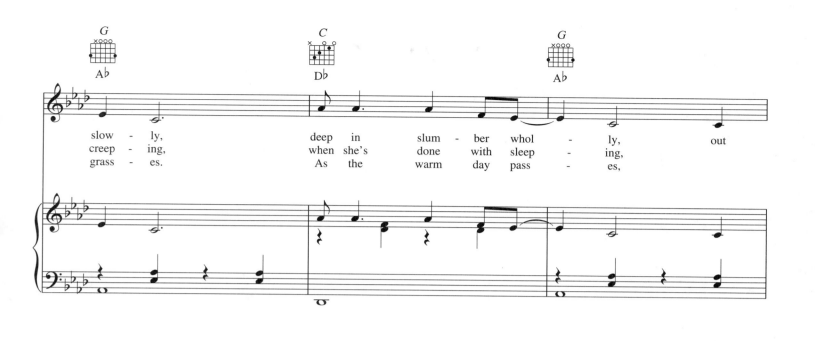

slow - ly, deep in slum - ber whol - ly, out
creep - ing, when she's done with sleep - ing,
grass - es. As the warm day pass - es,

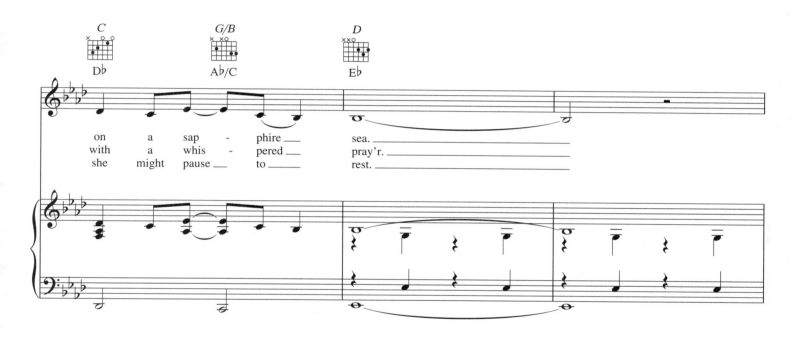

on a sap - phire ___ sea. _____
with a whis - pered ___ pray'r. _____
she might pause ___ to ___ rest. _____

On her lips, but bare - ly, a gen - tle smile ___ is
She goes to her win - dow as she's med - i -
I will walk be - side ___ her, hand up - on ___ her

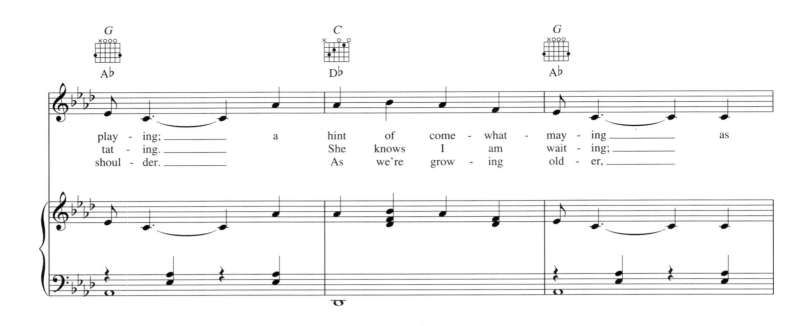

playing; _____ a hint of come - what - may - ing _____ as
tat - ing. _____ She knows I am wait - ing; _____
shoul - der. _____ As we're grow - ing old - er, _____

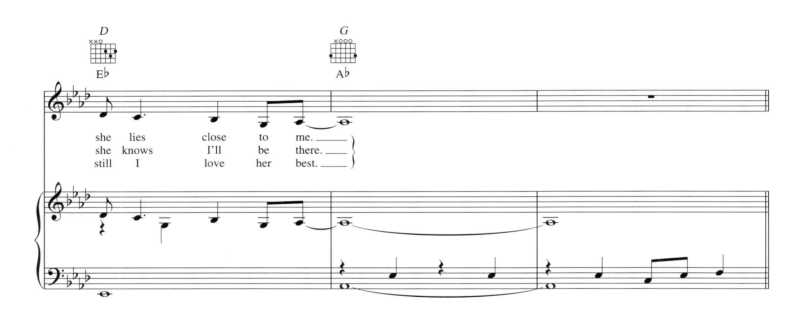

she lies close to me. _____
she knows I'll be there. _____
still I love her best. _____

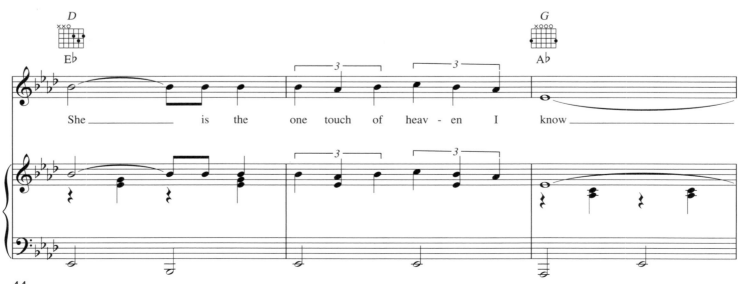

She _____ is the one touch of heav - en I know _____

I Like the Way You Look

Words and Music by
Tom Paxton

A Long Way from Your Mountain

Words and Music by
Susan Graham White and Tom Paxton

sun - shine on your moun - tain; you can see the world _ from there. You've got all _

_ the sky you want - ed; you get high _ on moun - tain air. _

You came down to Cam - den and you tried _ to make it go, but you dreamed _
Freight - ers on the o - cean sail - ing off _ to Liv - er - pool while the sea -

Now } I'm sit-ting on the coast ___ of Maine to-day, ___

sit-ting here ___ just throw-ing lit-tle rocks ___ in-to the bay ___ while the big ___

___ waves come in slow-ly, roll-ing strong and wild and

free. Oh, it's a long way from your

Home to Me (Is Anywhere You Are)

Words and Music by
Tom Paxton

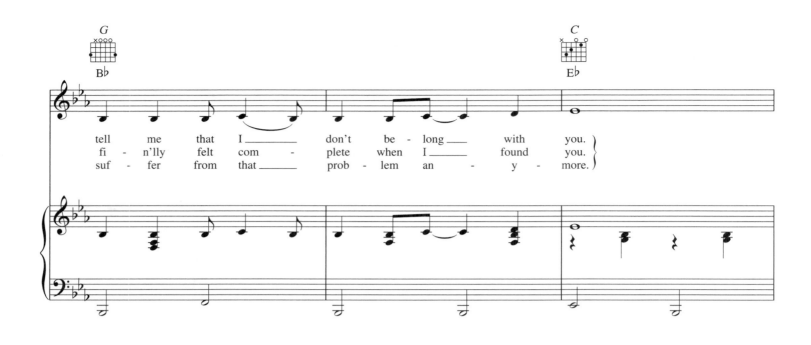

tell me that I _____ don't be - long _____ with you.
fi - n'lly felt com - plete when I _____ found you.
suf - fer from that _____ prob - lem an - y - more.

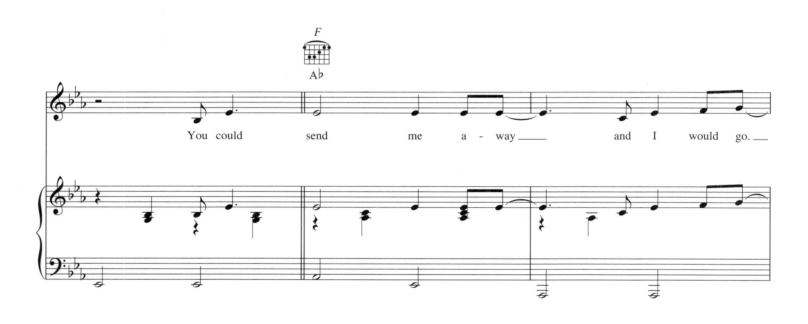

You could send me a - way _____ and I would go. _____

I would go, _____ but I

58

Jennifer and Kate

Words and Music by
Tom Paxton

things like shar - ing ___ feel - ings, ___ let's ad - mit they are not ___ great. But the

luck - y ones have daugh - ters like my ___ Jen - ni - fer and Kate. ___

Just

as they were as chil - dren, so they are as wom - en now. ___ So ___

62

heav-en on a plate. ___ For their ___ fa - ther thanks his an - gels for his

Jen - ni - fer and Kate.

Dance in the Kitchen

Words and Music by
Tom Paxton

Moderately, in 2

I love the can-dle-light, I love the soft vi-o-
Is-n't it strange how just a cou-ple of min-utes a-

lins. _____
go _____

I love the dark cor-ner ta-
I was all down in the mouth __

ble, the bot - tle of wine. _____
_____ a - bout all my af - fairs? _____

But when I'm hold - ing you just when the mu - sic be - gins, _____
Then two things hap - pened when I switched on this ra - di - o. _____

_____ hon - est - ly, dar - ling, the kitch - en will suit me just
_____ This song be - gan and, sweet dar - ling, you came down the

fine. _____
stairs. _____

Dance in the kitch - en, hon - ey,

dance to the ra - di - o. Glide 'cross the kitch - en floor; that's what they make 'em for. ___

We'll dance a - gain like we used to dance when love was new. ___

Come on and dance in the kitch - en. Hon - ey, I want to slow dance with

you. ___

You Are Love

Words and Music by
Tom Paxton

Comedians and Angels

Words and Music by
Tom Paxton

miss my friends to-night; ___ their fac-es shine ___ for me. The

clam-or of their sing-ing's like ___ some ___ mad cal-li-o-pe ___ still

75

me - di - ans and an - gels, __ I miss my friends to - night. __ I

won - der where they are __ now. They could be an - y - where, __ in

hell or Cal - i - for - nia or back in Sher - i - dan Square. __ They

left us where they left us so we'd put out the light. __ Co -

me - di - ans and an - gels, ___ I miss my friends to - night. ___

Each one drained the part - ing glass ___ and ___ sailed out to sea. ___ And ___

___ what a crew of rogues they made ___ in glee - ful an - ar - chy. ___ They